Am I

Trump?

Am I Trump?

The epitome of who I am or who we were...

Carter M. Head

Heads Up Publications

Atlanta

All rights reserved. No part of this book may be reproduced or transmitted in any form or by any means, electronic or mechanical, including photocopying, recording or any information storage and retrieval system without written permission of the author except for brief quotations used in reviews, written specifically for inclusion in a newspaper, blog, magazine, or academic paper.

Am I Trump?
Copyright © 2018 by Carter M. Head
Published by Heads Up Publications
Editor: Lashuntay Wilson
Cover by Pierre McCummings

ISBN: 978-0-9988323-2-6
Ebook ISBN: 978-0-9988323-5-7
Library of Congress Control Number: 2018946751

Heads Up Publications Books are available at special discounts for bulk purchases for sales or premiums.
Direct all inquiries and correspondence to:
Heads Up Publications
P.O Box 162593
Atlanta, GA 30321
e-mail: headsuppublications@gmail.com

Printed in the United States of America

This Book is Dedicated to:

NATASHA MOSELEY

PREVIN BLALOCK

WAHBA FRAZER

CAREEM MCKIBBEN

ZION BONNER

KAWHI JONES

Contents

Introduction................ IX

Foreword................ XIII

CHAPTER 1
   Facing the Mirror of Trump..............19

CHAPTER 2
   Am I Trump?...........................29

CHAPTER 3
   Trump's Center Stage Effect...............37

CHAPTER 4
   Mirrored Behavior..........................47

CHAPTER 5
   Lawlessness verses Liberty... Are we really getting away with it?................57

CHAPTER 6
   Reversing the Reflection..................75

Introduction

Allow me to be clear, our problems in this world is not the fault of one person and all negativity did not come from one President. Everything bad was not initiated by President Trump, this worlds issues are systemic. The negativity started from the beginning of human existence. We all have mental, psychological and social problems. This book will reveal that change will have to start with us as individuals. Allow me to present three disclaimers that this compendium does not promulgate: the first is, politics. I am not promoting any particular party or group. Secondly, this is not a book written to demean, shame or oppose the President of the United States of America,

President Donald J. Trump. I will always pray for him and for anybody that holds the office of the Presidency and I have a right to make a decision to agree or not agree with him. I will always respect the office of the Presidency and our democratic law makers. Thirdly, this book is not intended to be bias against whoever chooses to follow Mr. Trump.

My only motive and drive in writing this compendium is to be humble with reservation, influence and hopefully help to initiate the realization to all humans that each of us reflects some caricature or imagery of other human's personality traits. Some of those mirrored traits are negative and damaging to our society and humanity as a whole, in general aspects. When this awareness arises from the reading of this book, we all at that point will consider our secret and views towards one another that we all may portray or reflect a better race of humanity in which I am optimistic we will restore morals, values and a peaceful camaraderie amongst all humans for all of our benefit. I only ask you all to be honest within yourself whole heartedly, without reserve, please.

Foreword

This book fell into my hands at the right time. I was in the process of changing some of my feelings and how I looked at certain situations in my life. To be honest, I was struggling with mental war fares and didn't know where to start. By reading this book" Am I Trump", I was able redirect my thoughts and start in the right direction. This compendium really helped me to understand that we all have some work to do with ourselves. It also has helped me with my secret thoughts and how I felt about different people character traits. It's amazing how this book has changed my life. If you are serious about changing the way you feel and learning more about yourself for the betterment of humanity, you definitely have to dive in and read.

- ***Previn LaVell Blalock***
  Entrepreneur, Fire Fighter &
  Life Coach

This book is a tool that can be used in everyday life to help you understand who you are and help expose your secrets thoughts and to shed light on the thoughts that may be keeping us the human race from becoming one. This book is the future if we wish to evolve. It is a step towards unity by first encouraging us to work on us and to be less judgmental and more understanding of others.

When I first seen the title of "Am I Trump" I didn't know what to expect and I definitely didn't think my inner thoughts would get dealt with while reading this book. This book made me feel a little uncomfortable because it brought to the forefront some of the negative thoughts I have had in reference to people that I don't really know or didn't take time to get to know. I prejudged and made assumptions; yes, I am guilty so shame on me. One of my favorite parts in the book was the Behavior and Personality Traits Survey. All though they are yes and no questions they trigger other thoughts that really forces you to dig deep within. I have had a humbling experience while reading this book because it helped me recognize some things that I didn't know were there. We all need to recognize our ways and at least try on a daily basis to do better in whatever area that may be.

I remember an English teacher I had in my younger years saying, "a book is a ticket to another world." You can be locked up in a penitentiary but an author words can take you anywhere you want to be and can show you thing's in a different light. "Am I Trump?" has surely showed me things in a different light. I'm now addressing my negative thoughts and looking in the mirror. I realize understanding, love, empathy respect, and compassion for the greater purpose is what we all need to become one.

- ***Ms. Natasha Moseley***
  Investigator & Entrepreneur

1

Facing the Mirror of Trump

One of the most difficult and surreal events of our lives is actually looking into the imagery, actions and deep thoughts of our own personal character and behavior. The reason it is so hard to do so is because most of us fear what we already realize exist within our hearts. Some of what we think is very malicious, cunning, hateful and mean. We really do not want these aspects of our personality traits exposed for others to see especially on a broad platform in which many would see the negative part of who we are. So, we wrestle with the mere fact that we as individuals are two persons in one body in most cases. In which one is the good you and the other is the bad representation of you. We often attempt to keep the bad or negative personality at bay and present openly the good personality sometimes in order to get along with others in society.

This compendium will expose and also reassure us all of who we really are, why we may be that way and why we should change our ways. The way I choose to reveal this dilemma is by utilizing the mirrored platform of a person that we hear and see on a daily basis, whether it is through the media, internet or by association. By this person's character and personality which exposes his behavior will then when brought to our attention we all will see a few traits of his personalities are indeed some of our behaviors that we act out in secret. The person that reflects a lot of our secret thoughts or our past mindsets is the President of the United States, Donald J. Trump.

Be reminded President Trump is not the problem; most of all our behaviors, secret or opinion reveals a systemic problem that's been in our lives from the beginning of our existence on earth. Trump is only the reflection of our negative construct that is affecting all of us humans in a bad way. Know this, President Trump is not the only person on our planet that has personality and behavioral dissimulation. We all have personality flaws that need to be reevaluated, reconsidered and reconditioned in order to reappropriate the behavior God created within us all and that is love, peace, hope, assurance and joy in which all humans should desire to present openly and behind closed doors in order to reflect our true humanity towards all people. But again, to get to that point in life we must not be fearful and hesitant in realizing some truths about ourselves that most of us humans have been covering up. Yes, this will definitely be one of the most humbling fleets of our lives. But the rewards and benefits of revising our images will overwhelm us all with joy, peace, and tranquility amongst all of our fellow humans.

This book is only one tool that will hopefully initiate this new journey and new chapter in our life towards the goal of reconditioning, revising and recovering the true essence of all of God's Creation of Humanity. There will be segments of this book that will cause your head to tilt and your intellect to reject. But we all must at least consider the fact that we all need to change in some area of our behavior.

Trump is not the problem. Like Trump, we all are a product of the underlying problem. Trump's position and platform gives light to the problem and Trump is just a reflection of us all. And I see a reflection of negative and a reflection of goodness of heart and great accomplishments in him. Some of you may ask; What goodness? Well we must acknowledge his ability to seem sincere in helping others, his attempt to connect both parties and his accomplishments in overcoming opposition of his fellow Republican candidates being nominated as their Party's candidate and then President. Have Mr. Trump ever inspired Carter Head, yes definitely, by his ability to challenge Career Politicians and conquer one of the greatest offices in the world; President of The United States of America and also his boldness to speak his thoughts without reserve. I must say some statements he shares are sometimes reckless and demeaning and I do not agree with those type of caricatures. I am amazed with him expressing his truth and mindset. However, I am not his judge and jury, he's obviously operating in a mindset of liberty that most of humans are not comfortable projecting publicly.

We humans do not always want to acknowledge or face the fact that there is a source and reasoning for the bad or negative within us. This book gives us the opportunity to reconsider our ways. We all must wake up and change and do something about the negative in our lives, first acknowledging we all are a participant in the problem and as individuals, each of us must initiate a reversing of the reflection that Trump and others present in the mirror of our lives. After writing this book, I am no longer Trump. I am optimistic and hopeful that you as an independent individual, will govern and humble yourself; acknowledging to yourself in the mirror of your soul and mind that you now choose to change the image of lawlessness as I did. Maybe we will see a better image and reflection in the mirror tomorrow. Trump influenced me to repent and acknowledge my wrongs and change my secret thoughts from this day forward.

It is time for transparency. Could it be possible for other people to influence, conform and govern our lives by their actions and character? Can they also be a reflection of who we may have been or who we struggle not be now? For example, I love to eat food and I often overindulge in food and when I see my wife eating foods she should not partake in, it actually upsets me. Because to see her overindulge in food as well makes me feel guilty because she is doing something that I do too, that I should not be doing. When I see and hear people doing and saying things that I either have said, thought or done that are negative and wrong, it disgusts me to know I am possibly like that person. I now acknowledge it is time for me to reverse the reflection.

2

Am I Trump?

The title of my book; Am I Trump, is not against Trump supporters and is not giving credence to all of his political views. This is not a political compendium. I am neither a Republican nor a Democratic. I am not writing this book to discredit or bash Mr. Trump in reference to his views, political or non-political, neither the way he conducts himself socially.

This book and its title, "Am I Trump?" come from the premise of characterization of Mr. Trump's personality traits, that maybe and are oftentimes the construct and character of each of our human behaviors. After observing Donald J. Trump with humility of heart, I was concerned that the images, words and convictions he presented were likened unto my own at certain traits in which I chose.

Am I Trump? Survey

You will definitely want to complete the Behavior and Personality Traits Survey of 16 questions to answer yes or no to. In order for this book to really enlighten us all and also give credence to this concern, along with the answer to the question: Am I Trump? If I am found to be such, what can I do to reverse that mirrored image of my secret character. Listen, no one has to ever know or see your answers. If needed, please write your answers on a sperate sheet of paper and just remember the count of the answers should be yes or no to the 16 questions. Again, I suggest you do not write answers in the book; because you surely may want to share this book with another associate of yours.

Behavior and Personality Traits Survey

Answer Yes or No to each question that applies to you personally and even secretly.

1. Do you have a desire to do a task well and take obligations to others seriously as opposed to disorderly?
   A. Yes   B. No

2. Do you have an active imagination, attentiveness to inner feelings, and intellectual curiosity?
   A. Yes   B. No

3. Do you enjoy being around people more than being alone
   A. Yes   B. No

4. Do you have an optimistic view of human nature and getting along with others, ?
   A. Yes   B. No

5. Do you tend to be moody, worry, experience high anxiety, fear, anger, frustration, envy, jealousy, guilt, depressed moods or loneliness periodically?
   A. Yes   B. No

6. Do you secretly or openly have lack of concern for the wishes or opinions of others?
   A. Yes   B. No

7. Do you have a habit of being independent and self – reliant and stress the importance and worth of each person pursing their own self-interest because every person is unique and have moral worth as individuals?
   A. Yes   B. No

8. Do you ever lie to yourself within yourself, about yourself?
   A. Yes   B. No

9. Do you believe that you can influence events and their outcomes?
   A. Yes   B. No

10. Do you ever blame outside forces for everything?
   A. Yes   B. No

11. Do you have an individual desire for significant accomplishments, control, mastering of a skill or skills, high standards, and having a determination to win?
   A. Yes   B. No

12. Can you be primed, induced, or influenced in a decision-making process?
   A. Yes   B. No

13. Do you have an undue awareness of yourself, your appearance and actions with the quality of your goals being carried out deliberately and full awareness?
   A. Yes   B. No

14. Are you confident in your own worth or abilities with self-respect?
   A. Yes   B. No

15. Are you complex and intense with a readiness to take physical, social, legal and financial risks for the sake of feelings and experiences?
A. Yes   B. No

16. Are you uncomfortable with a lot of your secret thoughts?
A. Yes   B. No

If you answered yes to at least half of the questions on this survey, you definitely want to read this book in its entirety please… Just know deliverance and reversing this reflection that most of us see in the mirror of Trump can be systemically changing each day.

3

Trump's Center Stage Effect

The performance of our lives, the characters that are on display seems to be taking over the show. These center stage acts and focal points are "Lies," "Hatred," "Drama," "Sexual Immoralities,", "Ugliness," "Addictions," and "Conspiracies,". Why aren't truth, honesty, joy, God, family, peace and giving not at our point of focus. Shouldn't we be presenting these characters loudly on center stage? Whether the characters be represented loudly through social media, news reporting, religious constructs, the big screen movies at theaters, TV and family gatherings.

    I believe one of the reasons truth is not center stage is because truth is sometimes more far fetched than fiction or more unbelievable than fiction. Why is this happening? Why do most people accept lies, hypocrisy, drama, hatred, sexual immoralities and ugliness over truth, love, peace and giving? Here is my answer to that: because the truth and doing right requires no intellectual reasoning, it leaves no doors open to even desire to oppose it. Also, I think because in most cases, it is more comfortable to accept and adhere to untruths rather the truth because that sometime pushes us to move from a place of complacency. If love is presented, why would anyone purposely within them self oppose love? Why would anyone in their right mind be in opposition of someone giving them things that are beneficial and healthy for the whole of Humanity? There would not be a reason to intellectually defy and not agree with peace being promoted. These are the attributes that should be center stage, but lack of accepting such behavior and personality traits on center stage obviously comes with doubt, lack of understanding and fear. Again, the fact of the matter is because most people in our world are consumed with propaganda of lies and negativity on a consistent basis all day every day.

The lying, the deception, the drama, the immoralities often override the truth; the love, the peace and take center stage in our lives and mindsets. Remember, we obtain 83% of information from what we see and 11% of information from what we hear. So, the airwaves or media services and TV have our center of attention. We must choose to reverse that imagery and put love, truth and giving on center stage. Also, let's learn and practice not judging others and practice not asking people what is wrong with them; instead, ask them what happened regarding this or that situation which involves them or possibly someone else.

If indeed, we have come to understand that we all have some character flaws. We must practice being mindful of who we watch, listen to and follow because that person and/or those persons may be a significant influence in our lives and mental development. Sadly, we must measure ourselves by negative content with the assurance that our inner moral compass will govern us to know the difference between the good content verse the bad influence. In order to reject the negative ways of others so their character will not mold our character. An old slogan once stated, you are what you eat. In other words, you may become who you choose to adhere to. Be reminded it is time to really know who we are, and what is in our hearts. We must desire to operate as loving, compassionate and giving human beings in order for this world to be a better place in which to live peacefully with all humans.

To be transparent, in fact I admit having said, expressed and acted in some of the behavior traits as he. I wondered why I was so uncomfortable when he expressed certain views. I come to find out as I pondered on different aspects of his words, Trump was indeed a reflection of my mindset at a particular time in my life and even somewhat today. I realized I actually was looking at an image of who I used to be mentally. Thus, coming up with this title "Am I Trump?" Oh my God! How judgmental are we as humans! Scientific studies prove we all as humans have most of all the same behavioral personality traits as Trump in some aspect and/or form. But most humans will not openly admit to it. Initially, I was so uncomfortable not receiving or understanding Mr. Donald Trump actions and words because I was ashamed of myself because I once acted in some of those same personality traits as Trump. However, today I am willing and excited to expose and help others with the wrongful negative personality traits of humans by judging and damning others. Could it be because they reflect and mirror who we really are in secret? Selah.

Be reminded I am not in any way propagating that he or I are right and just in our ways. But none of the other humans are either. We all need to consider our ways. I admit that some of my past thoughts and even some thoughts presently are unacceptable to me in my heart. I am here to address this issue, to stop judging others and to cease lying in the mirror. Also, to share in this book, we as humans should collaborate collectively and honestly in a valiant individual effort to reverse the reflection. Trump is not the only one needing a change of behavior; we all need to be continually, persistently, evolving to change our hearts. Learning how to love, honor, appreciate and respect each other's views, Ideas and beliefs without choosing to destroy, discredit, hate and ostracize others with different caricatures opposite of ours.

Reverse the reflections to all the people who say I am not like Trump. Maybe you are not, maybe you used to be or maybe you will be in the near future. What really matters is the fact that some of us have to reach that conclusion about ourselves, which leaves room for concern about whether we are judging, belittling, discrediting and pointing out the flaws out of any human being. Yet, not focusing on our own personal negative thoughts, illusions, misconceptions and bad behaviors. Or could it possibly be in accordance to us subconsciously housing reserve or acknowledging that just maybe have somethings that are not quite right within us as well. "Am I Trump?" is an caricaturization of the epitome and mirrored imagery or reflection of who we are or could become.

    Lets all start with a mindset of unifying in love and respect towards implementing what I have labeled "Reserve Reflection" by changing who we are for the betterment of Humanity and nature as a whole in order for all humans to be at peace within and prosper throughout. I humbly believe all of our past, present and future presidents will adhere to this.

4

Mirrored Behavior

Human personality traits and behavior traits are imbedded in all of our human psyche, you know the human soul, mind or spirit. These traits are also a part of our human subconscious, the part of the mind of which one is not fully aware, but which influences one's actions and feelings. Our behavior and personality characteristics actually belong to us as an individual. We all should be enthusiastic about understanding how these traits makes for the images we present to others.

Allow me to share a little information on why we act like we do: it is called behaviorism, which is a systematic approach to understanding the behavior of humans produced by a response to certain stimuli which is a thing or event that evokes a specific functional reaction like an inspiration in the environment, that's conducive to the five factors of the personality of humans. The five traits are as follows:

Conscientiousness: the personality trait of being careful, or vigilant, it implies a desire to do a task well and to take obligations to others seriously, efficient, organized as opposed to easy going and disorderly.

Openness to experience: having an active imagination (fantasy), aesthetic sensitivity, attentiveness to inner feelings, preference for variety and intellectual curiosity.

Agreeableness: a person with a high level of agreeableness and is usually warm, friendly and tactful, generally haves an optimistic view of human nature.

Extraversion: a behavior where someone enjoys being around people more than being alone and likes being the center of attention.

Neuroticism: people who are moody, have high anxiety, worry a lot, operate in fear, displays anger, experience frustration, envy, jealousy, guilt and depressed moods of loneliness.

Now you see why we need this book, it is to bring to our awareness the need for all of us to seek and initiate change in our personalities in order for us all to be better towards ourselves and especially other people. This is the doctrine that individuals best serve the public interest by pursuing their own self-interest. It is all about taking care of yourself and believes that every person is unique. It believes the more worth of individuals.

Let's go a little further in our assessment of a few personality traits in humans.

Authoritarianism: which is people having a strict obedience to authority at the expense of personal freedom, that have lack of concern for the wishes or concerns for others. Do you know anyone that operates like this in your religious or political affiliations?

Individualism: the habit or principle of being independent and self-reliant. It is a social theory favoring freedom of action for individuals over collective or state control, it stresses the importance and worth of each person.

Narcissist: a person that has an inflated sense of self-importance, moody, touchy, restless, aggressive, excitable, impulsive, active, optimistic, antisocial, carefree and one that's leadership is unstable. But then at times stable, mean passive arrogant, hateful; even peaceful at times, anxious, pessimistic and even love just to name a few. We all can agree a narcissist is definitely a character of sort.

Sensation seeking: a trait that's defined by the search for experiences and feelings, a complex and intense person with the readiness to take physical, social, legal and financial risk for the sake of such experiences. These are people like most of us varied.

Self-esteem: confidence in one's own worth or abilities, with own self-respect.

Self-consciousness: having an undue awareness of oneself, one's appearance, or one's actions and quality of being carried out deliberately and with full awareness.

Need for achievement: an individual's desire for significant accomplishment, one that masters skills, loves control, with high standards, intense, that puts forth prolonged and repeated efforts to accomplish something differently, the work with singleness of purpose, having a determination to win. This probably reads you up and down or maybe not.

Internal verses external locus of control: internal locus believes that he or she can influence events and their outcomes, while external locus blames outside forces for everything. Sounds like a family member or associate doesn't it or maybe not?

Regulatory focus: it is a goal pursuit theory regarding people's perceptions in the decision-making process that can be primed, induced or influenced.

On a separate sheet of paper, please consider taking a few minutes to determine and/or discover how any of these personality traits listed may relate to your overall behavior that you present to others openly or in secret. If there are any, please list any triggers that may cause any of these traits to fluctuate positively or negatively when you are in contact with other humans, discussion of particular subjects or interacting with various objects.

Here is another one of my motivations to write this book, to bring awareness to this fact, that we all are being influenced by others and knowing such we all need to reconsider our ways. Due to most of our influences comes by way of subliminals, propaganda, and mind control, indirectly or directly and our government along with the President is an intricate part of that influence being that most of humans are in this world hear, see and experience information being presented to us 7 days a week, 365 days a year, 366 days when it's a leap year and most of the time it is showing caricatures and behaviors that are branded into our psyche even our subconscious, maybe at times unknowingly. These events develop our personality and behavior traits in some form or fashion.

Again, after realizing this fact, we must all reevaluate our own character and how we actually treat others and how we present ourselves in this world. We must ask our self the question "Am I Trump?" in some aspect of some of or at least one of his personality traits and if you indeed you answered yes to more than half of the questions from the survey, it is a great possibility you act and think like President Trump in some ways or fashion. If some of his ways bother you maybe it is because you and I look like and think somewhat like Mr. Trump. So, no not only does Donald J. Trump need to change some of his ways. But we also need to change some of our ways of thinking and acting.

Think about now; could Trump's reflection actually be projecting the images of our inner thoughts?

5

Lawlessness verses Liberty... Are we really getting away with it?

Is liberty with boundaries freedom? We have to address this in order to understand whether or not we have the ability to choose not to be lawless. People tend to always justify the wrongs they are doing because it becomes more and more comfortable to live a lie because the truth is much more harder to live because the truth brings us out of our comfort zone. The truth brings us all into a place of light and exposure. So, it is much more easier to lie about a truth. When we are living a life of lying about what is actually true with complacency, peace and ease it only solidifies we may be a lawlessness person that's been conditioned to really believe it is normal in which the false impression of liberty and freedom exist in that person's mind. I call it being free to operate in lawlessness. We must face the good and bad part of ourselves. One of the hardest things to do is to look ourselves in the face. It is very difficult to expose yourself to truths in reference to self, from a negative image of how you act or used to act.

It is very concerning, how much information we receive from the portals of our eyes and ears. Neuroscience and cognitive psychology research uncovers the power of our senses, most neuroscientist say we receive 83% of information from sight (what we see) and 11% from our ability to hear. So visual and auditory portals are virtually important to how we obtain information that helps how we think and reason. These two portals are an intricate part of building our behavior and personality traits. Who we listen to and watch the most could possibly be who we trust and mimic. If this is the finding, most of us are actually mirroring one another. So, you or Trump may be a true reflection and imagery of a part or percentage of my or your secret character. That may be the cause of many of us getting upset with other actions and ways. Could we be subconsciously saying I really do not want to be like that anymore or remind us of a personality trait we displayed in our past?

It is past time for us all to start the process of reversing some ugly reflections. In order to properly address this dilemma of liberty and lawlessness we must adhere to the information I am about to share on Free Will verses Determinism. Many have interpreted having free will as being the ability to only focus on the good of what we are doing but ignoring the wrong. So, I submit a question: are we really free moral will agents as a human species, when there is always within our self the concept of law?

Let's deal with this with all honesty and sincerity of heart. Could it possibly be we are just pretending to be free, knowing deep down inside we do not have liberty in what we are doing. This is a part of the reasoning we all must face, realizing by watching and hearing the ugliness of others as a mere reflection of what we are actually thinking and doing secretly in most cases. It is so easy to criticize Mr. Trump and others we observe acting negatively, but at the same time ignoring that what they are doing and saying mirrors our own mindset and actions. Maybe having free will gives us all the right to judge but not be a judged. Maybe it also gives us the right to criticize others for what we are doing in secret. This is what I have labeled **<u>thought and irrational thought</u>**: this is a principal that says an action is free only if the person doing the thing could have done otherwise. But don't we all have this liberty to do anything we want? I beg to differ because though an act of free will comes at one's own discretion, it should always be with constraint. Being that no human is to their own and are not of their own, with all of our actions there is a cause and effect on others. So again, should we all be at liberty and effect on others just because we are free to do so? If we are at what cost, then? Patrick Henry once wrote "give me liberty or give me death." I wonder did he really choose that slogan with the understanding of its severity and wide range of interpretation. The way I understand it now after writing this book; is to be free to do what I want even if it causes my demise and perhaps the death of others as well.

Give me liberty or give me death is an irrational thought that we are free to things. But shouldn't it come with law, structure and guidelines from a moral thought, realizing whatever I am free to say and do could affect others negatively. Shouldn't there be a moral law within my psyche that governs me with rational? I am not actually dealing with libertarians or liberals, remember my disclaimer in my introduction at the front of this book. I am addressing the systemic overlooking of morals just because we declare freedom to do as we please. To be liberal is to be open to new behaviors or opinions and wiling to discard traditional values. I am only saying that is fine, but at what cost?

Are we as a human race willing to and ready to suffer the consequences of not confronting our own mirror that reflects the lawlessness of most of our actions? There has to be a governing force to help us all before it goes too far. I believe that force to be embedded in the human perception of morality. We do have options and the ability as humans to choose and make decisions in reference to our personality and behavior. It just need to be emphasized sometimes to remind us that in our society there is still good and bad behavior and we should all digress and humbly reconsider our own actions, ways and affect on others. Shouldn't we care? We are living in a time on earth that there is a state of disorder due to a disregard to the law, we live in a world full chaos, crime, unruliness and anarchy.

Look at the governments all over the world, full of confusion and unconcern for their fellow man or women. Is lawlessness misconceived liberty and freedom that is justified? Who decides is it a president, a religious leader, our guardians or maybe you and I? Henry David Thoreau once quoted, "any person more right that their neighbors can constitutes a majority of one already." So, I ask should one person speak for all of the human race? Should one person be the reflection of all humanity? Or maybe it is possible for one person to be the catalyst, a person that precipitates the event of reasoning and reevaluating our thoughts and behaviors? I say yes. Trump is not the problem but a reflection of many of the systemic problems we as human have had throughout history.

This book is a vital part of helping us to fix it before it's too late. Are we a product of Determinism, the doctrine that all events including human action are ultimately determined by causes external to the will? Some philosophers have taken determinism to imply that individual human beings have no free will and cannot be held morally responsible for their actions. I believe we are obviously going fast in that direction. A French philosopher stated, "none of our actions are actually free because everything is the inevitable result of what came before us including everything that we do." But I say without reserve, we must violate determinism and rise above subjectivity, being influenced by personal feelings, taste, opinions and perceptions by opposing the wrongs of it using our moral instinct. Knowing I do not have to be like the negative image that have been formed from generation to generation. There is a freedom to change in accordance to knowing right and wrong. I do understand that what we see, hear, eat and who we associate ourselves with, does help develop our personalities. We also have the ability to recognize the wrongs coming from those entities but choose to not be conformed by them when it blatantly denotes bad.

It is time to stop being afraid and apologetic in reference to right, law, structure, guidelines, stipulations and pretenses. Being lawful, doing what is right and discrediting a lie have all gotten a bad rap. Just know truth, regulations and doing right by no means are designed to destroy any freedom we have, its only a means by which we are governed so that we can destroy Humanity. But live peaceably almost each other and until we all adhere to these moral laws already written on the tables of our consciousness and hearts we all will be subjected to disorder, confusion, disobedience and early demise of the human race.

Doing right morally will not put us in bondage or restrict our livery to be free as humans with intellect new ideas and input on the decision-making processes in this world. Matter of fact doing right morally will enhance our human ability to understand that God created us and enables us all to operate in liberty and freedom with desired guidance. We then having a feeling about doing what is good not only for us as individuals but also for the whole of Humanity. This is the moral compass that's been hidden deep inside our race of humans for so long, being subjected to so many lies, falsehoods, religious views, politics, racism, hatred and selfless behaviors.

Now I am hopeful and optimistic that the true essence of human values is coming back to the forefront of our intellect and hearts. I really believe in the human race and our ability to strive, obtain, refrain from and change for the better. We need laws, lets never misinterpret lawlessness and bring freedom to do as we please without repercussions. Lawlessness is a state of disorders of the law, wickedness and uncontrolled by a law, full of chaos and unrestrained behavior. Misconceived freedom has given power and the right to act, speak and think as a person want as one without restraint in their own choices or actions.

Remember liberty and freedom has to be governed by moral law at least. This does not mean being conservative is the only solution; because conservatives are averse to change and hold dear to traditional attitudes and values. Most of the time being cautious about change and innovation this concept is what makes for the producing of liberals who are open to new behavior and opinions and are willing to discard traditional values. This is where most of the conflict and misrepresentation of freedom and lawlessness stem from. We must have a common and moral approach to this dilemma. Realizing our new ideas and our old traditionals can come to a common place through reasonings together with moral empathy, respect, love and compassion for the greater purpose and that is to assure all of humanity of a better life, full of joy, hope and prosperity.

Freedom if utilized and presented morally is the equivalent to bring happiness in liberty having peace in whatever we do or will do with the sensibility of law whether moral or civil. St. Augustine once quoted "An unjust law is no law at all." We all have the freedom to also reject or denounce that civil law, but none of us humans have a right to deny moral law because it comes from our conscience. Knowing this I declare freedom and I am liberated. Even though we all can choose to debate whether to obey or not obey a law, moral or civil we should be aware of this truth; nothing should be able to abrade or gradually destroy the moral guidelines or rules of law, no matter how technical, spiritual, political or intellectual the argument is.

    Civil laws can be flawed from a social, economic, political and spiritual connotative and we should continue to be at liberty to discover the flaw and change it when those laws are not conducive to the productivity of a more better way of life equally for all humans. Civil laws are also the law of God but sadly some law maker interpret the concept of law from a self-motivated stance leaving the concept of a creator God out of the equation. There are consequences to breaking those laws. We have to adhere to all laws until they are changed. I am not here to give you a lesson on law. I am writing only to prompt your awareness that doing wrong should bother us all and we realize we are uncomfortable in what we do and how we act that probably is our moral instinct kicking in. We should take notice and stop rejecting and overlooking the unctionings that knows we can do different and do better in that particular situation. Whether that is in the area of your health, relationships, careers, schooling, habits, self-promotion or spiritual enlightenments.

    Remember moral is always the key to peace and camaraderie for all. Never allow anyone, not even your president or leader to convince you to do wrong when you know the difference between right and wrong. It is okay to do right. It is okay to change from our old ways and promote peace for all.

6

Reversing the Reflection

Trump maybe the epitome of who we are, who we used to be or possibly who some us will be influenced to become. After reading this book you as an individual will have to decide whether or not its okay to think like, act like or mirror the personality and behavioral traits of President Trump or not to want to have the mentality and personality as Trump. Its been proven in this book that each of us at some time in life personify certain aspects of his character even if its only in our secret thoughts, behind closed doors. Saying things, he says only within the confined of our homes. We must admit also that some of us are guilty of acting like Trump and processing some of his ideologies in which we only share amongst our peers and close associates.

Whatever area of imagery of likeness we share with Trump by now is recognizable and we are more than likely ready to change or reverse that image when its been found to be negative because remember I have shared that President Trump definitely has some good aspects and intentions about a few things as well and I agree with him in those cases. I am only advising you to examine your own heart in reference to whether or not the negative behavior he presents resemble who you are and what you think. If so its time for change. Is past time to start reversing that mirrored reflection. You have to make that choice on your own because if you leave it up to your associates they probably will not acknowledge your wrongs, yours flaws and/or your bad habits.

Some of the reasons why are as follows:

    A. They do not want to hurt your feelings.

    B. You may end your association with them.

    C. They try to respect your opinions and the way you say and do things even when they know you are wrong.

This is why often the people we are close to will turn a blind eye to our wrongs in order to either agree or cover up the negatives about that particular subject matter. Some people will not tell us the truth about ourselves in order to save face and continue to get things from us and often for the keepsake of our company because their connection with us makes for the possibility of them having a better life. When our close associates do not bring the things, we do that are bad to our attention they become contributors to the same negative behavior. So, this makes it even more important that you initiate the change in your own life first. We all should see the error of our ways prior to someone telling us.

To change or turn from the image and reflection of the negative personality and behavioral traits we have, we must first feel uncomfortable with the way we act and think. If you are not bothered by your immoral mindsets, bad ways and/or secret thoughts you probably will not change. You may think you are okay the way you are, obviously you do not believe you are flawed, but all humans are. Time for all of us including Mr. Trump to change and reverse the negative images we have been presenting. Only then can we start the healing process among the human race.

It is always good to be persistent in being the best you that you can ever be because evolving into a greater aspect of you will definitely be an intricate part of a better significant society. The nice part of this change will come with all of us unifying on a better plateau in peace and tranquil for all. My prayer for us all, is that you accept this book as an objective read that will prompt us to a place of not returning to the bad, problematic, ugly, side of our past negative behavior and personalities. Finally, realizing that the former mirrors of like behavior represented by and through each of us at one time or another are distilled and removed once and for all. Some may say "yeah right, wishful thinking." No, I am seriously optimistic and hopeful that all humans are not only subject to eventually change, but many are inspired to change.

I know people can change, I have. I have admitted my like behavior as Trump. It lead me to seek change and all I desired to do was to reverse that reflection I was viewing in my mirror acted out by Trump in some areas of my life. I am here to share with you all my bad behavior has changed for the better and I am constantly addressing my personality flaws. I see much better days ahead with connecting with all others from all different nationalities, religious sect, political practices and gender with being bias towards them. We all are works undone, we are now humans in the working. God speed in your effort to do the same as I.

If you are serious and ready to reverse the bad images you have been reflecting, start now. Now is the ideal time in order to assure your part in the reconstruction of our human race. Having all negative, immoral, irrational, damaging persons abolished leading to peace on earth and good will towards all people. *Consider taking the following steps*:

1. Admit I need change in some of my ways.

2. Read this book over again.
3. Seek counsel or therapy in some cases. (Only you know the severity of your actions.)
4. Recognize change will not come in your life on its own you have to do something about it.
5. Limit as much as possible negative conversations about other people.
6. Do not be hard on yourself. Change takes time and consistency.
7. Pray and ask God to grace you to see the good in all people.
8. Spend less time watching tv, being on social media, viewing news channels, being consumed

with religious rituals and traditions. (I did not say you had to stop being involved in areas listed for #8, just do not allow it to be your only focus) Also, be aware that there is a lot of propaganda out there on the internet and all media sources, even music.

9. Obtain a copy of the book Lying Mirrors by Carter M. Head. (It will help with any identity crisis you may have)

10. Never give up on you!

Just know you do have the power to reverse the reflection of your life at any time. Practice some of these steps every day and it will make for a better you and a better world.

Peace & Love,

Thanks for your attentiveness as you read this book.

Authors Final Suggestion

On our quest to be at peace with the era of divisions, hatred, opposition and a Trump governing force, allow me to suggest a way to alleviate the frustration most of we humans have with one another. Trump is not the only person that offend people with his words. Many people we all come in contact with on a daily basis tend to at times offend us and our stance or ideology. Sometimes we allow them to get us upset because we are holding on to and analyzing every word that proceeded out of their mouth. May I recommend a solution to this dilemma that is causing all of us to become even more divided and hateful towards one another. A lot of the confusion is due to lack of understanding, misunderstandings and misinterpretation of another's thoughts and reasoning of their heart in what is being said.

Please let's consider or maybe assume that much of what Trump says maybe does not or possibly could not come from his heart but from his head and influence of his counterparts, constituents, confidants and just lack of knowledge in some areas. We all are flawed in some aspects of our lives in reference to our perceptions of one another. Maybe many of us are over observant, watching and listening too hard to President Trump every word, thus judging him accordingly, to the point of allowing our mindsets, emotions and understandings to be prompted and governed by every word, sentence and statement he makes. Most are so focused on him to the point of even watching his hands, the tone of his speech, the way he communicates and even his body language. Why?

Mr. Trump and all the other people that we see and listen to are flawed and we say things sometimes we do not mean from the heart. We all are human. I do understand some of his words matters and we should be concerned and interested in the President of the United States conversation and actions. But not to the level of allowing what ever he says to affect us to the point of administering hatred towards others to the point of whatever he says upsetting us so much that we walk in frustration, anger and stress all day, every day, because most of us are holding on to every word he speaks that's excessive and its hurting us as individuals, mentally, sometime physically and even spiritually. We must calm down.

There's a professor of psychology, Albert Mehrabian who constructed a study called the 7-38-55 rule; this study shows that only 7% of what we say is communicated by the words we use, 38% of what we say is communicated by our body language, and 55% of what we say is communicated by the tone of our voices. I have also in accordance with his research, come to realize that most of what we as humans say derives from the thoughts, influences and actions of others, not all from our own hearts. So, we all as humans should take what we hear from others with caution and reservation, knowing not all is truth that comes out of the mouth of others. Also knowing that what others say is mainly opinionated conjecture and all of us are intitled to our own perceptions assumptions and opinions.

It is time to stop taking others we communicate with and people we associate with and people we see on social media and tv so serious all the time. Holding on to every word they may say allowing what is being said to dictate and conform our emotions actions and behavior because in doing so this causes many of us to condition ourselves with hatred, anger, offence, bewilderment and stress. Thus, causing some of us to suffer medical, psychological, and physical complications.

Yes, we should continue to consider a person words and their ideologies or stances in order to better make a choice to connect or not connect with them, but never to this point. We must not allow Trump's words or anyone else words divide us as human because a lot of what Mr. Trump says is not based on facts and I choose to believe that some of what he says comes not from his heart, but from his hand, his lack of understandings the influence from others he's connected to. Again: cease being offended by choosing to hold on to every word that comes out of people mouth. Practice to not be so easily offended because of the words that others speak. Choose peace within and peace amongst all humans.

About the Author

Carter M. Head is a life coach, a minister, and is one of the most dynamic, realistic, and sought-out conference speakers. Carter is a graduate of Andersonville Theological Seminary and Alumni of West Georgia College. Carter founded and established many outreach organizations in reference to feeding and clothing the indigent. Carter also established the YL2 (Youth Leadership League of Henry County, GA), and he coproduced three live stage plays emphasizing on the issues of our youth. Carter established the mentoring group called B.I.N.O. In addition, Carter is an author, grant writer, marriage counselor, and philanthropist.

Other Books by the Author

- ◊ Lying Mirrors
- ◊ Unity for What?
- ◊ Questions with No Answers

www.ingramcontent.com/pod-product-compliance
Lightning Source LLC
Chambersburg PA
CBHW050442010526
44118CB00013B/1647